Max on Life

PARTICIPANT'S GUIDE

Max on Life

PARTICIPANT'S GUIDE

Based on the DVD featuring *New York Times* Best-Selling Author

MAX LUCADO

PREPARED BY RANDY PETERSEN AND PAUL LANUM

THOMAS NELSON
Since 1798

NASHVILLE   DALLAS   MEXICO CITY   RIO DE JANEIRO

Published in Nashville, Tennessee, by Thomas Nelson. Thomas Nelson is a registered trademark of Thomas Nelson, Inc.

The publishers are grateful to Randy Petersen, Paul Lanum and Jackie Mosley for their writing assistance and collaboration in developing the content for this guide.

Thomas Nelson, Inc., titles may be purchased in bulk for educational, business, fund-raising, or sales promotional use. For information, please e-mail SpecialMarkets@ThomasNelson.com.

ISBN: 978-1-4185-4755-4

Printed in the United States of America

11 12 13 14 15 RRD 5 4 3 2

Every page of the Gospels hammers home this crucial principle: God knows how you feel. From the funeral to the factory to the frustration of a demanding schedule, Jesus understands. When you tell God that you've reached your limit, he knows what you mean. When you shake your head at impossible deadlines, he shakes his too. When your plans are interrupted by people who have other plans, he nods in empathy. He has been there.

—Max Lucado

❧ CONTENTS ❧

❈ INTRODUCTION ❈

Pastors receive many letters. Writers are asked many questions. Being both a pastor and a writer, I've heard more than my share. And they've shaped my thoughts. Genuine questions have determined my radio messages, sermons, books and this video series.

Trace the ancestry of my lessons to their beginning, and you'll find a humpbacked punctuation mark: "Max, can I ask you something?"

We've created a question mark to highlight our questions. It's stooped and bent, perhaps because questions can leave us in the same shape, burdened and weary. We have deep, heavy questions. We pepper our questions with *whys*, *whens*, *whats*, and *how comes*.

We crave answers. Straighten this mark, and let it stand. Replace the cowering curl with a confident exclamation point. Easier said than done.

Some questions defy easy answers. But you know that. You've been looking. I know that. I've been looking as well.

Like autumn leaves on soil, these wonderings tend to sit and sink in until springtime emerges and I have a thought or two. This Bible Study series collects some of those thoughts.

Many of these answers appeared initially in earlier books. Others are only now being heard. But all of them, I pray, will help you with your questions.

By the way, thanks. Thank you for opening the door to your heartaches and concerns. You've told about your struggles and shared your joys. You've welcomed me into your lives. I am honored to walk the path with you.

After all, aren't we in this together? (Another good question.)

Max Lucado

9

❧ HOW THIS STUDY WORKS ❧

Life is really complex. We face challenging situations at home, at work, and at church. We struggle in our families, marriages and with our children. And sometimes things happen that just don't seem to make sense. As a result, we have questions. *Why is this happening to me? Where is God during my suffering? Is there any hope?*

In the next 4 weeks, you'll hear real stories from people who are wrestling with some of life's most challenging questions. Max Lucado will take you to God's Word to find some answers to these difficult questions.

In the group discussion after the video, there are questions to help you connect the video to your own emotions or experiences and you will be led through passages of Scripture to grow in your faith together. Throughout the guide, you will find blocks of text, which are quotes taken directly from the *Max on Life* book.

Each week also includes five days of reflective reading. You'll do this part of the study alone during the week, after you have watched the video. You will want to have a Bible and pen in hand. You will find a few special sections spread throughout the readings as well. "Inspiration to Change" will challenge you to reconsider how you think about and act on certain biblical ideas. "In this Together" will give you the opportunity to use what you've learned to make a tangible difference in someone else's life.

Your group may be brand new or have years of connection. Whatever the case, use this *Max on Life* study to take things to the next level. Share from your heart on the questions raised. Be open with each other as you struggle to find answers. Encourage and pray for each other throughout the week. And stay in God's Word.

> *Knowing God is like mountain-climbing. Some days the path is steep. Others, the trail is easy. Clouds can eclipse the view. The sun might illuminate the peak. Most of all, it just takes time. Know this: God will help you.* —Max Lucado

WEEK
I

❧ HURT ❧

For our light and momentary troubles are achieving for us an eternal glory that far outweighs them all.

— *2 Corinthians 4:17 NIV*

❊ INTRODUCTION ❊

Why do we suffer? It's probably the toughest question we have to face as believers. And it's not just some theoretical quandary for scholars to bat around, but something that touches our lives deeply. If we believe in a God of love and power, why can't God use his power to keep bad things from happening to us? It's a complaint as old as Job.

We've all gone through tough times, and we've all asked the question: "Why me?" It's hard enough to deal with calamity but it makes it even worse when we don't understand why it's happening. In today's video, Max Lucado explores these tough questions.

A lesson like this won't provide all the answers, but it might lead us into a tighter embrace with God.

❊ ICEBREAKER ❊

What do you do in your daily work? What sort of preparation have you gone through to do that? Note that "daily work" involves whatever someone spends most of the day doing. For a student, it's school. For a homemaker, it's the home, or the family. Preparation can be anything—education, past experience, a personality trait, or a lucky break.

❄ VIDEO NOTES ❄

❈ AFTER THE VIDEO ❈

We saw two very different real-life stories in the video, though both involved a great deal of personal pain. Rob was accused of something and dismissed from his job, putting his family in a very difficult financial situation. **How would you feel in a situation like that?**

Max zeroed in on the issues of anger and hurt. He suggested three things to do in situations like that.

1. *Change your focus.* **It's easy to say, "Let God be your focus," but how can you do that?**

2. *Discover why a person behaves that way (their past).* **Are we making excuses for a person when we try to understand their past?**

3. *Pray for the person who hurt you.* **Have you ever prayed that good would come to a person who hurt you? What happened?**

Jennifer was struck by a life-altering disease, and she shared her reactions in brutally honest ways. She mentioned some "cutting things, just insensitive things, Bible verses" that Christians said to her. "It's such a strange thing that scripture can hurt sometimes." **Have you ever been hurt by people who were trying to comfort you?**

Is there anything you could say to Rob, Jennifer or someone like them that would help?

Read 2 Corinthians 4:8–10. The apostle Paul is writing from his own experience as a missionary. **In what way does Paul "carry around . . . the death of Jesus"? Could we say the same thing about ourselves? How is the "life of Jesus" revealed "in our body"?**

Someone go back and read verse 7. **Why has God entrusted his great treasure to our clay jars?**

Read 2 Corinthians 4:16–18. **How can we "fix our eyes ... on what is unseen"? How can that help when we are in times of hurt?**

Read 2 Corinthians 5:1–5. **What does this passage say about our "purpose"?**
What is "this very purpose" (v. 5)?

How could this sense of purpose help us when we go through painful
circumstances on earth?

> "Consider it pure joy, my brothers, whenever you face
> trials of many kinds, because you know that the testing
> of your faith develops perseverance. Perseverance must
> finish its work so that you may be mature and complete,
> not lacking anything."
> (James 1:2–4 NIV)

❧ Reflective Reading ❧

Day 1: No Revenge

Blood ran down his forehead and dripped off the end of his nose. He watched as it landed below in a pool of red now forming in the brown dirt. His arms ached. Splinters of wood lodged themselves in the fresh wounds on his back as he slowly slid up the plank, trying to catch his breath.

He gathered his strength, raised his head, and looked out at the faces staring back at him. Some people gawked at his naked body. Others mocked him, calling him names. Down to his left, several soldiers were arguing about who'd get his clothes. People he had never seen before hurled insults at him. "Criminal! Liar! Blasphemer!" they yelled.

Right in front, the priests and leaders responsible for putting him in this disgraceful position grinned with smug contentment. But he was innocent. Not once had his lips spoken falsely. Not once had he acted out of selfish ambition. Not once had he disobeyed God's law.

But instead of putting his accusers in their place, he raised his head heavenward and said, "Father, forgive them, for they do not know what they are doing" (Luke 23:34 NIV).

When someone hurts us, our natural instinct is to hurt them back—to defend ourselves—especially if their outburst is unprovoked and undeserved. But that's not how God wants us to respond. We are called to follow Christ's example.

Read 1 Peter 2:19–25.

Consider the last time someone wronged you. How did you react? How do you think you'd have reacted if you were in Jesus' situation? What do these verses teach us about the importance of the words we speak?

We might be tempted to dismiss this call to follow Jesus by pointing out that he was God, so of course *he* could endure unjust suffering. But Jesus was also fully man. The key to understanding how he could endure this kind of abuse is found in his purpose, for Christ endured the humiliation of the cross so that he could extend grace and salvation to us. How might you endure suffering and thereby demonstrate God's grace to someone this week?

Never, never have I seen such love. If ever a person deserved a shot at revenge and had the power to do some serious supernatural damage in the process, Jesus did. But he didn't call down armies. He called down grace. He died for them.

—Max Lucado

Day 2: It's Worth It

Few things tax a woman's body like pregnancy. Soon after hearing the good news, you're as sick as sailor in a cyclone. Your body starts to expand in gravity-defying proportions and your skin begins to stretch farther than your budget. You walk the aisles of the grocery store on swollen feet looking for chili cheese-flavored corn chips—and you don't even like chili—while children stare at the unusual shapes the alien in your abdomen is creating through your clothes. And then at 2 a.m., after shopping online at Land's End for a new wardrobe, you finally begin to drift off when a circus erupts in your stomach.

Then there's the pain of delivery, that first diaper change, and nights of even less sleep. As you warm her 4 a.m. bottle, your whole future blurs before your eyes—brawls over makeup and short skirts, sneaking in late through the bedroom window, and the pain of watching her go off to college where you can't protect her anymore. At some point you wonder why anyone ever bothered to reproduce.

But then, those tiny fingers curl around yours and the crying subsides as a little miracle falls asleep on your chest. Soon, pureed peas get used as hair conditioner and your home is filled with innocent laughter. Before you know it, she's off to her first daddy-daughter dance after catching the game-winning pop fly. And then you realize—it's all been worth it.

While not everyone experiences the pain of childbirth, we all endure hurts and heartaches of one kind or another. Jesus was well familiar with the suffering people face and began the Sermon on the Mount by reminding us of the eternal rewards that await those who endure persecution for him. One day, we too will say, "It was worth it."

Read Matthew 5:1–12.

Jesus says nine "blessed are" statements in this passage, and at least three of them directly involve some sort of human suffering. What might that proportion indicate about normal life? What pain are you experiencing right now? And what promise can you see in these verses?

Contrary to expectation, Jesus instructs us to "rejoice and be glad" when we endure hardships (verse 12). How does his promise of "great reward in heaven" color the way you see your current condition? Take some time to write out below an honest prayer to God about how you feel in your present circumstance. Consider how you might use these verses to encourage someone you know who is grieving or oppressed.

INSPIRATION TO CHANGE: LOVE IS NOT A FEELING

Jesus was radical. Everywhere he went on earth he challenged the conventional thinking of the day—and of ours! On one particular incident he dropped this bomb, "Love your enemies, do good to those who hate you, bless those who curse you, pray for those who mistreat you" (Luke 6:27–28 NIV).

It's easy for us to read those words and agree in our minds, but it's a whole different thing to put Jesus' teaching into practice. In Luke 6:27–36, Jesus provides several concrete things we can do to "love our enemies."

As you go through the list below, it may help to think of someone you are struggling with right now. But before you do anything, ask for God's guidance. Loving your enemies doesn't come naturally; it requires supernatural strength.

- *Pray:* When was the last time you prayed for that overbearing boss or temperamental neighbor? How about the police officer who gave you a speeding ticket?
- *Give Freely:* Who owes you money? Could you cancel their debt? Tell them they don't have to pay you back; it's a gift. Or, generously meet a need of someone with whom you are at odds. Try and do it without them knowing.
- *Do Good:* Are you and your neighbor not on speaking terms? Take them a meal. And the lady that cuts in front of you at the gas station—surprise her by paying for her gas.
- *Turn Your Cheek:* Has a co-worker been taking credit for your work? Let it go. Did someone in your small group criticize your cooking, again? Resist the urge to retaliate.
- *Bless:* It hurts to hear someone say unkind or untruthful words about you. Instead of returning insult for insult, find something kind to say to them— something that will encourage and build them up.
- *Love:* Treat others the way you want to be treated. How would you feel if your "enemy" approached you and apologized? What if they offered to make amends, no matter the cost? Now stop thinking, and do it.

DAY 3: FORGIVENESS

Our Father which art in heaven,
    Hallowed be thy name.
Thy kingdom come,
    Thy will be done in earth,
    as it is in heaven.
Give us this day our daily bread.
And forgive us our debts,
    as we forgive our debtors.
And lead us not into temptation,
    but deliver us from evil:
For thine is the kingdom, and the power,
    and the glory, for ever. Amen.
          Matthew 6:9–13 KJV

Children often learn the Lord's Prayer as one of their first assignments in Sunday school. It's so familiar that many of us can recite it by memory. But how often do we pause to consider its meaning?

Nestled in the middle of the prayer, Jesus inserts a profound truth about forgiveness. It's so important, that Jesus takes a moment to clarify his thoughts before moving on. In Matthew 6:14–15, Jesus tells his disciples, "For if you forgive men their trespasses, your heavenly Father will also forgive you. But if you do not forgive men their trespasses, neither will your Father forgive your trespasses."

At first glance we might conclude Jesus taught that in order for us to experience God's forgiveness in salvation, we must forgive others. But the Bible is clear that salvation is a gift of God's grace by faith, and our works play no part in it (Eph 2:8–9). In addition, when God saves us through Jesus' sacrifice on the cross, he forgives all our sins—past, present, and future (Col 2:13–14; 1 John 2:2).

Instead, Jesus spoke about our ongoing relationship with God. If we refuse to forgive others, then our relationship with God is hindered. Our unforgiving attitude accentuates our lack of appreciation and understanding of how much God has forgiven us. But when we realize the significance of our sins against God, and the high price he paid to redeem us—the death of his Son—we are compelled to forgive the offenses others cause us, which by all accounts are trivial in comparison.

Forgiving others allows us to see how God has forgiven us. The dynamic of giving grace is the key to understanding grace, for it is when we forgive others that we begin to feel what God feels.
—Max Lucado

Read Matthew 18:21–35.

First-century rabbis taught the Jews that they needed to forgive someone who committed a repeated sin against them three times, but no more. Peter radically suggested pushing that limit from three to seven. But Jesus responded that forgiveness has no limits. Think about your own life. Are there areas where you've created "limits" to your forgiveness?

While this passage challenges us to freely forgive others, it also reminds us of God's limitless forgiveness toward us. We *are* the servant, begging before the king for mercy. Start each day this week by thanking God for "canceling" your debt.

Day 4: No Stunt Double

Have you noticed that in action-adventure movies, the hero and villain can fight forever in grueling hand-to-hand combat—absorbing devastating blow after blow—and yet still remain standing? In Hollywood, actors work with stunt doubles, fight choreographers, and skilled makeup artists who apply the minor cuts and scrapes they appear to receive during combat. But in reality, most fights are over quickly since the human body can only withstand a certain amount of pain.

You get that same "no way!" feeling when you read what the Apostle Paul endured in his lifetime. Paul was beaten up repeatedly, near death constantly, flogged five times with thirty-nine lashes, caned three times, stoned and left for dead, shipwrecked three times, and abandoned in the open sea for a night and a day. He endlessly warded off robbers and enemies who sought to destroy him, was sleep deprived and hungry, and was often left exposed to the scorching sun and freezing winds (2 Corinthians 11:23–27). And Paul didn't have a stunt double. If there was one thing he knew, it was suffering.

Yet even in the middle of all this torture, Paul wrote, "The sufferings we have now are nothing compared to the great glory that will be shown to us" (Romans 8:18 NCV). As difficult as it is to endure present day hardships, God promises that when we stand before him in heaven, all our earthly troubles will seem inconsequential compared to the glory that we share with him.

Read Matthew 10:16–31.

Like Paul, the other disciples Jesus sent out also experienced great suffering. That doesn't sit well with us. We run from suffering. We crave comfort. But what do these verses suggest that we should expect if we follow Christ? What do verses 24 and 25 tell us about one reason why we suffer? And how should we react (verse 26)?

Even though we experience pain, Jesus reminds us that God cares deeply for us and is in total control of every situation on earth, right down to the moment when a small bird flies its last. How does realizing that God knows and commands every detail—including the abundance or absence of hair on your head—change the way you view your current distress? This week, memorize Matthew 10:28–31. Take a moment and write it out below. Recite it to yourself when you feel your trust in God begin to wane.

In This Together: Comfort Others

Their brother, whom they dearly loved, was terribly ill. Since they knew Jesus cared for him, Mary and Martha sent word to Jesus to come quickly. But just after the messenger left, their brother, Lazarus, died.

They carefully wrapped his lifeless body in strips of cloth and with the help of several men from their town they laid Lazarus in a tomb. Grief pierced their hearts. But there was still hope, since Jesus was bound to come as soon as he heard the bad news.

A day passed.

And then another.

Lazarus had been well liked in the Jewish community and many people had come to help comfort Mary and Martha. But one person was notably absent, which made their grief even more unbearable.

Jesus finally arrived after Lazarus had been dead for four days. He saw Martha first, since Mary was too distraught to leave the home. After he spoke a few comforting words to Martha, Jesus asked about Mary.

As Mary reached Jesus, she fell weeping at his feet. He looked down and saw her pain. He looked around at all the people who were there sobbing with Mary and Martha. And then Jesus wept.

What's remarkable about Jesus' reaction—that he paused to grieve with the others—is that he already knew he was going to raise Lazarus from the dead. Days before he returned to Bethany, he told his disciples that he would bring Lazarus back to life (John 11:11). And yet Jesus doesn't march in and tell everyone to dry their eyes and stifle their sniffles. With deep compassion, Jesus joined in their pain and mourned the loss of this dear brother.

Is there someone you know who is in pain? This week, follow Christ's example and comfort someone who is hurting.

Maybe you are struggling yourself. But reaching out to someone else will put your woes into perspective. Maybe you don't know what to say. That's okay. Just sit and listen.

You might be tempted to preach to this person all the tremendous truth you've learned in this lesson this week. Don't. It is usually enough to *be with* a suffering person, to *listen* to them, to *show you care*, to *pray* with them (if they want, and keep that simple too). If there are words you need to say, pray that the Lord will guide you to say them.

> The Lord is a shelter for the oppressed,
>   a refuge in times of trouble.
> Those who know your name trust in you,
>   for you, O LORD, do not abandon those who
>   search for you.
>
> (Psalm 9:9–10 NIV)

DAY 5: CRASH LANDING?

Colossal earthquakes. Tsunamis that decimate entire towns. Nuclear radiation. Hate crimes. Human trafficking. Wars in the Middle East. Suicide bombers. One look at earth today and you're convinced the pilot has abandoned the plane and we're all headed for a disastrous crash. But it isn't so.

Scripture confirms that God is in control (Isaiah 45:9–19). He not only created everything in existence (Hebrews 11:3), but he also controls the weather (Psalm 135:5–7), rules over the nations (Psalm 22:28), and decides when, where, and how long every person will live (Acts 17:24–28; Psalm 139:16). In fact, God commands it all (Psalm 103:19).

Yet as we sip our coffee and scan the headlines, we struggle to understand why God allows such rampant evil to persist. Why doesn't he stop all the senseless violence? How can a loving God allow such tragedy? Why does it seem that wickedness is winning?

While we may never find answers that completely satisfy all our yearnings, our future is certain. The Book of Revelation confirms earth's final destination, and the destiny of all who believe in Christ Jesus. Even though, as passengers, we don't completely understand all the intricacies of the flight plan, we can still trust the Captain to bring us in for a safe landing.

Read Romans 8:18–39.

As we look around at the world, things look broken. They looked broken to the Apostle Paul too. Two thousand years ago Paul wrote that all of creation groans under the consequences of sin and eagerly waits for God to put things right. Take a moment to consider what life will be like once God rights all the wrongs and redeems the universe. How can this hope change the way you live today?

Paul assumes that life will be filled with trials (verses 35 to 39), but is confident that we will emerge as conquerors. Paul assures us that nothing, including future events, will separate us from God's love. What guarantees our ultimate triumph (verses 32 and 34)? What are the implications of God adopting you as his child (verse 23)?

> *From our perspective, the world looks like chaos. From God's, it's all going according to schedule. From our perspective, evil is center stage. From God's, evil is taking a selfish bow during its final act.*
> —Max Lucado

WEEK
2

❧ HIM/HER ❧

Love must be sincere. Hate what is evil; cling to what is good. Be devoted to one another in love. Honor one another above yourselves.

— *Romans 12:9—10 NIV*

❋ INTRODUCTION ❋

Marriage can be one of the most incredible and rewarding experiences on earth...but it can also be very hard. The stresses and difficulties of our lives invade any marriage. Couples might argue over money, sex, kids, schedules, habits, or expectations. Even in healthy marriages, there is conflict.

In difficult times, some couples grow closer together; others see their relationship shatter. How can you handle the daily difficulties without weakening the relationship? And when a marriage has taken a hit, is healing even possible?

In today's lesson we'll take a no-nonsense look at our marriage relationships, and we'll see how faith and forgiveness can keep us together.

❋ ICEBREAKER ❋

Have you ever joined anything? Is there some group or organization, a club or team you have joined?

Why did you join? What benefits did the group offer?

What sort commitment was necessary to be part of this?

❧ Video Notes ❧

❧ AFTER THE VIDEO ❧

We saw two stories of couples who had gone through major difficulties in their marriages. Todd and Lisa fought over finances and eventually went into counseling to work some things out. Roland and Cynthia struggled to heal their marriage after her affair. **What phrase or quote from their stories most stood out to you? What would you tell them if they came to you for advice?**

Max Lucado suggested five things that a couple could do to strengthen a marriage.

1. *Be considerate.* **When is it most difficult to be considerate to your spouse? What are some specific ways to show consideration?**

2. *Keep courting.* What do you think Max means by "courting"? What are some "challenges" to courting? What are some specific ways to keep courting?

3. *Fight fairly.* Shouldn't we stop fighting? Fair fight or not, is it better not to fight at all? What does it mean to fight fair?

4. *Lock the escape hatch.* **What does that mean? In your opinion, how can a couple stay ahead of the pressures that can slowly erode a marriage?**

5. *Ask Christ to place his Spirit within you.* **Specifically, *how* can our faith in Christ help us have stronger marriages? How has it helped yours?**

Max had an interesting set of questions for couples who were dealing with an affair.

1. Have you failed your spouse?
2. Has your spouse failed you?
3. Have you failed yourself?

What do you think is the hardest—confessing, forgiving, or dealing with your own guilt? Why?

Read 1 Peter 3:8. **Peter gives us five things to "be"—which do you find especially interesting? Or especially challenging?**

Can you give a real-life example of one of these qualities *in a marriage*? How did that play out?

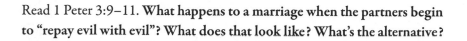
Read 1 Peter 3:9–11. What happens to a marriage when the partners begin to "repay evil with evil"? What does that look like? What's the alternative?

In an effort to "seek peace and pursue it," is it better to avoid talking about things you have a problem with? Should you keep your complaints to yourself?

Let's consider several complaints we might hear from a husband or wife. **Based on the verses we just read, how would you respond to a Christian saying any of those things?**

1. "I'm putting a lot into this marriage and not getting enough out of it."

2. "I hate to say it, but my love for my spouse has faded."

3. "I can't bring myself to forgive this. My spouse doesn't deserve to be forgiven."

If we want to be like Christ in all our relationships, but especially in our marriages, how can we do that?

What are some specific ways we can pray for each other in our marriages?

"Love is patient, love is kind. It does not envy, it does not boast, it is not proud. It is not rude, it is not self-seeking, it is not easily angered, it keeps no record of wrongs. Love does not delight in evil but rejoices with the truth. It always protects, always trusts, always hopes, always perseveres."

(1 Corinthians 13:4–7 NIV)

❈ REFLECTIVE READING ❈

DAY 1: CONSTRUCTION CRANES

What is your natural communication style? Are you like an express train, talking non-stop without pausing to pick up new passengers? How about a missile, waiting dormant until you ignite and blow up? Maybe you're more like a hybrid car, gliding along without making a sound. We each have a habitual style of communicating with others—especially with our spouse.

But as we continue to grow in our love for God and each other, God challenges us to put aside what comes naturally and become people who communicate grace, love, and encouragement. The Apostle Paul wrote, "Do not let *any* unwholesome talk come out of your mouths, but *only what is helpful for building others up* according to their needs, that it may benefit those who listen" (Ephesians 4:29 NIV, emphasis added). Basically, God wants us all to communicate like construction cranes.

High above the construction site, the tower crane lifts massive pieces of steel. Every beam is carefully chosen and skillfully fitted into its proper place. If the work is done well, an impressive structure begins to take form. But if the crane operator is careless, one dangling hunk of metal becomes a wrecking ball, destroying months of work. Likewise, the words we choose to speak to our mate have the power to build up, or the power to destroy.

Are you carefully building your structure?

Read Ephesians 4:25–32 & Psalm 4:4.

Paul writes against speaking deceit or falsehood (verse 25). Is that really an issue in marriage? Don't husbands and wives know each other completely? In the context of marriage, how would you define "unwholesome talk" (verse 29)? What sort of talk *should* we be engaged in?

In verse 26, Paul quotes a sound byte from Psalm 4:4 and then adds his own comment about dealing with anger before nightfall. What does this verse tell us about how to deal with our anger? What sort of "foothold" do we give the devil when we hang onto rage? What specific guidance does Psalm 4:4 give us?

Take a moment to look honestly at your own communication and write a prayer of confession for any times you may have used communication to tear down rather than build up. As a forgiven person, make a commitment to make amends.

> *You may be the first person to rebuild the encouragement foundation of your house, but it's a positive first step. Remodel now, and pick the new pattern of speaking that will decorate your home forever. Remove the weeds, and allow the sweet-smelling flowers of love to bloom.*
>
> —Max Lucado

DAY 2: TEAMWORK

Have you ever wondered why God chose to take a rib from Adam when he created Eve? What's wrong with part of a femur or clavicle? Or why not make her out of the dust of the ground, just like he did Adam? The 18th-century minister Matthew Henry pondered God's choice and wrote in the well-known *Matthew Henry's Commentary on the Whole Bible*,

> ... the woman was made of a rib out of the side of Adam; not made out of his head to rule over him, nor out of his feet to be trampled upon by him, but out of his side to be equal with him, under his arm to be protected, and near his heart to be beloved.

No, God did not create an upgrade—man 2.0—or an alien life form. Instead, God created Adam's perfect human complement—a companion to stand by his side. God designed them to work together as a team to care for the garden oasis in which he placed them (Genesis 2:15, 20). And even after sin, which destroyed their idyllic Eden, God's desire for marriage remained the same—a man and a woman, side-by-side, facing the joys and challenges of life together.

Like earth's first couple, our spouse was also designed by God to complement us. We have our differences—physically, relationally, and in responsibility—but God still wants us to navigate life together: hand-in-hand, protecting our marriage, and loving with all our hearts.

Read Genesis 2:20–25.

Why do you think it's important for a man and woman to leave the comfort of their parents' homes to begin life together as a new family unit (verse 24)? Have you done that in your own marriage? Is becoming "one flesh" just referring to a physical connection, or are there psychological and spiritual implications to this verse? How can you be a better team player?

The New Living Translation begins verse 23, "'At last!' the man exclaimed." Adam is excited. Note, he did not ask God to make her taller or change her hair color. He rejoiced in the marvelous gift God gave him. Think back to when you first fell in love with your spouse. How can you thank God, today, for the good gift he has given you in your mate? Write down what you appreciate in your spouse. This week, find a way to creatively express your appreciation for your spouse. Be specific.

INSPIRATION TO CHANGE: IMITATING CHRIST

When looking for role models in marriage, the best example to study is Jesus Christ. The Apostle Paul even compares marriage to Jesus' relationship with the church in Ephesians 5:22–33. Understandably, writers have penned a lot about marriage based on these verses. We often, however, overlook other passages that describe Jesus' actions and attitudes when seeking instruction for marriage.

Paul also wrote Philippians 2:1–11. These verses are full of marital significance. Let's look at five key character traits we find in Christ. Ask yourself, "Do these qualities characterize me?" and "How will growing in these areas impact my marriage?"

- *Tenderness toward your mate:* Men usually don't brag about being tender. But it's an important quality Christ modeled for both husbands and wives. Being tender means more than tearing up at an insurance commercial—it impacts the way you speak, touch, and think.
- *Consider your spouse better than yourself:* For some of us this is easy, since we clearly married above our pay grade. But the real issue is pride. Humility disarms discord. Let him load the dishwasher his way and listen to her when she tells you to turn left.
- *Look out for his or her interests above your own:* Most of us are preoccupied with ourselves. So the first step is focusing our attention on our spouse. What do they enjoy doing? Join in with them—cheerfully— even if it isn't "your thing." What needs do they have that you can meet? Be extravagant. Christ was.
- *Serve them whole-heartedly:* The God of the universe "...did not come to be served, but to serve..." (Mark 10:45 NIV). If Jesus came to serve your husband and your wife, so can you.
- *Love them enough to die for them:* Most of us will never have to literally perish for our mate. But we can still put to death bad attitudes and selfishness. Loving your husband or wife includes surrendering your self-will for their benefit.

Day 3: Your Secret Life

Thoughts—you can't taste them, touch them, or smell them. But the secret broodings that rattle around in each of our heads have a profound impact on the reality we experience—with God, at work, and at home.

The Bible confirms the tragic influence an unguarded thought life can have on reality; "All these evil things begin inside people, in the mind: evil thoughts, sexual sins, stealing, murder, adultery, greed, evil actions, lying, doing sinful things, jealousy, speaking evil of others, pride, and foolish living" (Mark 7:21–22 NCV). There are few "instant" sins; most are cultivated in a lush garden of mental iniquity.

In the context of marriage, we often focus on our actions toward one another more than our thoughts. And while what we do is vital to the health of our marriage, so is what we think. Smiling at your wife in her new dress while thinking, "You're fat," will eventually hinder your relationship. Hugging your husband as you repeat in your mind, "I can't wait for you to go to work," plants the seeds of strife.

Fortunately there is a cure. And that cure begins with fixing your thoughts on Jesus.

"So all of you holy brothers and sisters, who were called by God, think about Jesus, who was sent to us and is the high priest of our faith."
(Hebrews 3:1 NCV)

Read Philippians 4:8.

Paul points to six things that are excellent, praiseworthy, and worth thinking about. As you read the words below, consider how—in your marriage—you can practice focusing on each one. Be specific.

What is...

- True

- Noble

- Right

- Pure

- Lovely

- Admirable

Sometimes the truth is difficult. All of us, including every husband and wife, are sinners. Paul isn't suggesting that we ignore one another's sins. Elsewhere he wrote, "Make allowance for each other's faults, and forgive anyone who offends you. Remember, the Lord forgave you, so you must forgive others" (Colossians 3:13 NLT). What sins of your spouse do you still need to forgive? How can you concentrate on the positives, and not the negatives?

Make it a priority this week to forgive something small that your spouse does—but don't talk about it. This exercise is not meant for major misdeeds, just a lateness, an inappropriate comment, a silly oversight, something like that. In your own heart, just decide to let it go. You might say a silent prayer: "Lord, you have forgiven me much: help me forgive this little thing."

> *You will live tomorrow the thoughts you tolerate today. Use this to your advantage! Want a stronger marriage tomorrow? Ponder the strengths of your mate today. Want to enjoy more faith tomorrow? Meditate on God's Word today. Desire a guilt-free future? Then saturate the present in grace. You are what you think.*
>
> —Max Lucado

DAY 4: DON'T SHARE

Ever since you were young, you've been taught to share. Share your toys with the neighbor. Share your bedroom with your brother. Let your sister borrow your sweater. Even John the Baptist's parents taught him to share. He said, "If you have two shirts, share with the person who does not have one. If you have food, share that also" (Luke 3:11 NCV).

But there are some things you absolutely should not share. Your toothbrush. Your prescriptions. And your spouse. When you get married you join an exclusive club—a club with only two members. Your club has no wait list and no room for mixed doubles. And the clubhouse is never open for others to drop by and inquire about membership.

King Solomon, considered the wisest man to have ever lived, understood the importance of exclusivity in marriage. In Proverbs 5:15–17 he wrote,

> Drink water from your own well—
>> share your love only with your wife.
> Why spill the water of your springs in the streets,
>> having sex with just anyone?
> You should reserve it for yourselves.
>> Never share it with strangers. (NLT)

But like many today, Solomon failed to follow what he knew to be right. He married hundreds of women and kept plenty more on the side. In the end, his unrestrained sin led him away from God and brought dire consequences (1 Kings 11:1–13).

Read Proverbs 5:15–23.

While Solomon wrote this proverb to his son, the truths are equally applicable to women. What does it mean to be "captivated" by the love of your spouse (verse 19)? How can you "rejoice in the [spouse] of your youth"? Are you looking only to your mate for physical satisfaction?

In the verses preceding these (Proverbs 5:7–14), Solomon describes the consequences of unfaithfulness: wasted years, lost wealth, remorse, public humiliation, and utter ruin. As if these weren't adequate incentives to avoid adultery, he adds four more in verses 21 to 23.

- God sees everything—we have no secrets from him.
- God examines our conduct.
- Sin captures us and confiscates our freedom.
- Lacking self-control leads to death.

Read through this passage with your spouse. Take a moment to recommit yourselves to each other before God. Write out what that will look like in your relationship.

In This Together: Sing a Song

Song of Songs, the twenty-second book of the Old Testament, doesn't get much airtime. The author used complex Hebrew that is difficult to translate and employed highly figurative language—some of which seems mysterious to us today. In addition, most people are pretty sure it includes numerous references to sex, and so it just doesn't get discussed much in mixed company.

But God knew what he was doing when he included this beautiful chapter in his great book (and when he created sex). Like no other, the Song of Songs captures the sheer joy and delight of marital love. In a graceful frolic, Solomon and his bride exchange words of passion, longing, and anticipation. She delights to be in his company and he rejoices when they exchange their vows (Song of Songs 2:3; 3:11). It's impossible to read through this song without noting the sense of joy the couple finds in one another.

And that's something most marriages could use more of—joy.

This week, choose one or all of these activities.

Three times this week, find something that delights you about your spouse and say so. Be creative. Why not compose a song? How about writing a short poem? You could text a special message.

Twice this week, spend time reading Song of Songs together as a couple. The book has eight chapters, so you can easily read it in two sittings of four chapters each. You might even take turns reading the parts to each other. Spend some time discussing what you just read. How do the words make you feel? What images does the text bring to mind about your own relationship?

Once this week, go on a date with your spouse. Or at least reserve a time to do something fun at home. This does not need to be a time to "talk about our relationship." Just enjoy being together.

DAY 5: ARRANGED MARRIAGES

The thought of our parents picking out the person we are to marry is enough to make some of us shudder. Countless questions come to mind. "How will they know if we're compatible?" "What if they're ugly?" "What if I don't love that person?" But statistics suggest that many people today aren't that successful at picking mates for themselves. Maybe the problem isn't in the selection; maybe it's in the execution.

In Old Testament times, parents usually chose whom their children would marry. Although the child's wishes might be taken into account, as were Rebekah's (Genesis 24:58), the final decision usually rested with the father. Part of the reason this system worked was because their concept of love was different than ours. One Old Testament scholar wrote, "They did not marry the person they loved; they loved the mate they married."[1]

Feelings took a back seat to honor. Beauty acquiesced to responsibility. Priority rested not on the romance of courtship but on the devotion of marriage. The new couple celebrated their union, but always understood that they remained under the careful authority of the groom's father.

In truth, we're not that different. The next time you look at your spouse, consider that your heavenly Father just might have arranged your union. And as much as we like to think we're in control, in reality, we too are under our Father's authority—bringing honor to the family when we remain steadfastly loyal to our mate.

[1]Youngblood, Ronald R., F. F. Bruce, and R. K. Harrison, eds. *Nelson's New Illustrated Bible Dictionary*, Rev. ed. (Nashville: Thomas Nelson Publishers, 1995), 804.

Read Romans 12:9–16.

Notice the number of words that imply endurance. Cling...devoted...honor...
never lacking...keep your spiritual fervor...patient...faithful. How do these
verbs help you define the sincerity of true love (verse 9)? What value do you
think God places on persistence in marriage?

Paul writes, "Be joyful in hope, patient in affliction, faithful in prayer" (verse
12, NIV). How can you be joyful with your spouse this week? If a difficult
situation comes up, what can you do to practice patience? How often do you
pray *for* your spouse? How often do you pray *with* your spouse? Talk with your
spouse about committing to pray together at least three times this week.

> *Love is not a feeling. Love is a commitment.
> Thankfully, God does not love me based on whether
> he feels I meet all his standards. He loves me because
> he promised to love me in sickness and in health,
> for better and worse, for as long as we both shall
> live (which is eternally). And God always keeps his
> word.*
>
> —Max Lucado

WEEK

3

❧ HOME ❧

Love the Lord your God with all your heart and with all your soul and with all your strength. These commandments that I give you today are to be on your hearts. Impress them on your children. Talk about them when you sit at home and when you walk along the road, when you lie down and when you get up.

— Deuteronomy 6:5–7 NIV

❊ INTRODUCTION ❊

The greatest joys and worst sorrows of our lives possibly happen in our homes. Bringing up children is a major challenge, and everyone worries that they're doing it wrong. Discipline is fraught with difficulties—how much is too much, or too little? And how can we nurture a genuine faith in our children? The task is so great, there's no doubt we need divine help.

Of course one of the ways we learn about parenting is from the way we were parented—both good methods to re-use and bad ideas to avoid. Many people talk about how their parents messed them up, but parents also do many good things, and it helps to remember these as well. Families face big difficulties in the modern age—single parenting; step-parenting; moving; the fast pace of our weird, wired world; the permissiveness of our culture broadcast through a zillion channels; etc. Parents are always second-guessing themselves, even when they seem to be doing pretty well.

This session is about learning, not about guilt. We need to get past the blame game and get smart about the daunting process of healthy home building. Perhaps Max Lucado's advice in this video will give you new ideas, or maybe it will affirm what you're already doing.

❊ ICEBREAKER ❊

What kind of kid were you growing up? Were you cute and sweet, or a holy terror? Were you obedient or rebellious . . . or sneaky? What do you remember?

Looking back, what can you see that your parents did right? Was there a good piece of parenting that you remember? Was there a bad piece of parenting to avoid?

❊ Video Notes ❊

❧ AFTER THE VIDEO ❧

We heard from Michelle, the mother of a rambunctious five-year-old who felt like a failure. **Have you ever felt like this as a parent? If she was your friend and she asked you for advice, what would you tell her?**

Max Lucado had five pieces of advice. **Give some specific examples of how you carry out each of these. Do you struggle in any of these areas?**

1. Be careful.

2. Be consistent.

3. Be clear.

4. Be compassionate.

5. Be close.

What did he want parents to "be careful" about?

Max identified two different types of misbehavior in children: oversights and rebellion. What's the difference? How should they be dealt with?

Max made the point that children might make bad decisions or do bad things, but they're not "bad" themselves. How is this a helpful distinction?

The second mom, Vicki, talked about a heartbreaking situation that's all too common: A child who grows up and forsakes the faith. **If she was your friend and she asked you for advice, what would you tell her?**

The daughter's withdrawal began in her teens, but now the daughter is about thirty. How does a parent's input change over that time? **What can you say to a 16-year-old that you can't say to a 30-year-old, and vice versa?**

Read 1 Corinthians 13:1–3. Spend a moment to create a "parenting version" of 1 Corinthians 13:1–3 verse by verse and be specific. Write it out using examples of good parental duties and religious training that are not worth anything without love. **What do you think of that? Is that a fair adaptation of parental love?**

Read 1 Corinthians 13:4–7. Take a look at the list and let's take some time to think about how each of these descriptions of love would play out for parents. **How would a parent show love in this way?** Jot down your thoughts. Be as specific as you can be. Take a few minutes on your own and then we'll talk about your answers.

Love . . .   **What it looks like for parents**

is Patient

is Kind

does not Envy

does not Boast

is not Proud

Love . . .   **What it looks like for parents**

is not Rude

is not Self-seeking

is not Easily Angered

keeps no Record of Wrongs

does not delight in evil
but Rejoices with the Truth

Love . . .   **What it looks like for parents**

always Protects

always Trusts

always Hopes

always Perseveres

"But as for you, continue in what you have learned and
have become convinced of, because you know those
from whom you learned it, and how from infancy you
have known the holy Scriptures, which are able to make
you wise for salvation through faith in Christ Jesus."

(2 Timothy 3:14–15 NIV)

❧ REFLECTIVE READING ❧

DAY 1: GOLDFISH

Your son takes aim. And with one precise toss of a ping-pong ball, you become the owner of a small goldfish.

"Let's call him Lightning," your boy says as he proudly holds up the clear plastic bag.

Having never owned a fish before, you stop at the local pet store on the way home from the fair. You learn that goldfish like the water cold—around 68°—and can grow to about six inches long, so they need a decent-sized tank. As you load the ten gallon aquarium, the glow-in-the-dark plants, the sunken pirate ship, the coral reef tunnel, the dark blue gravel, the water conditioner, the test kit, the fish food, the pH balancer, the slime-coat remover, and the biological bacteria-booster into your trunk, you try not to think about the $85 you just spent on a 27-cent goldfish.

Once home, you carefully clean the tank, pour in the water, arrange all the decorations, start the filter, and then check the water again before depositing Lightning into his new home. It seems like a lot of work to keep one small fish alive. But if you aren't careful to maintain a healthy tank environment, you'll end up running back to the pet store while your son is in school to look for another 27-cent goldfish that looks exactly like Lightning.

Unlike goldfish, children are priceless. But they too need a carefully maintained home environment in order to flourish. Part of our role as parents is to provide for the physical needs of our children. But God charges us to nurture them psychologically and spiritually as well (Deuteronomy 6:4–9; Proverbs 22:6). Nothing is more important than encouraging our children to have a personal relationship with Jesus Christ. And God knows no human is more effective at fostering that spiritual relationship than a child's mom and dad.

Read Deuteronomy 6:4–9.

The order of these verses is very important. What does God direct us to do, as parents, in verses 5 and 6? Then, what are we to do (verse 7)? Why is this order so important? Four verbs are used to indicate when parents are to talk with their children about God and his ways—sit...walk...lie down...and get up. How often do you discuss spiritual things with your children?

In response to these verses, the Israelites were taught to wear small leather boxes containing scrolls of parchment on their heads and arms—called tefillin—and attach a small decorative case containing a piece of parchment inscribed with Deuteronomy 6:4–9—called a mezuzah—to their doorframes. These remind them of how God miraculously delivered the children of Israel out of bondage in Egypt (Exodus 12–14). What visible reminders of God's saving grace do you have in your home?

> *Make your home a place of grace. Young people mess up . . . and when they do, moms and dads, let's give them a safe place to land. Let's give our children what God gives us: clear teaching, appropriate correction, and abundant forgiveness.*
> —Max Lucado

DAY 2: HEART TREASURES

The Bible doesn't say much about Jesus' childhood. He was born in Bethlehem and, after a detour through Egypt, grew up in Nazareth (Matthew 1–2). The only other event mentioned before he began his public ministry as an adult is a trip he took with his parents to Jerusalem at age twelve (Luke 2:40–52). Scripture does not elaborate on the particulars of their return trip, but it may have unfolded something like this.

Mary and Joseph had enjoyed the eight-day Passover festival but were now tired and eager to begin the long trip home. Mary double-checked the ropes Joseph had used to secure their belongings to the donkey—didn't want a repeat of last year's fiasco with their personal effects dumped all over the road—while Joseph was off confirming the route home with their relatives.

The group started home, and everything seemed to be going fine until Joseph asked, "Where's Jesus?"

"I though he was with you," Mary replied.

"No. I was supposed to get directions, remember? You were supposed to find the kids," Joseph said.

Afraid and frustrated, Mary and Joseph made a sharp u-turn and headed back to Jerusalem to locate their son. When they finally found Jesus three days later, he was unharmed and talking with priests and teachers of the law in the temple court. Although relieved, Mary scolded Jesus for causing her and Joseph to be sick with worry. Jesus calmly responded with something about already being in his Father's house, but that made no sense to Mary. "Then [Jesus] went down to Nazareth with them and was obedient to them. But his mother treasured all these things in her heart" (Luke 2:51 NIV).

What an interesting conclusion to this episode in Jesus' life. Mary *treasured* these things in her heart—the joy of being reunited with her first-born child, the angst of not knowing where he was, and the pride of watching him amaze scholars four times his age. Imagine the other moments of Jesus' childhood that Mary had the privileged of experiencing. Were these the moments Mary clung to as she watched her son die on the cross? Did these heart treasures comfort her during the many years after Jesus' resurrection and subsequent return to heaven?

What treasures are you storing up in your heart?

Read Luke 2:40–52.

These verses suggest a slight tension between Jesus' desires to continue to obey his earthy parents while furthering his relationship with Father God. We know that Jesus never sinned (Hebrews 4:15), so this tension is not bad. As your children grow, what tensions—good and bad—will they experience? How can you help them navigate the transition from being completely under your authority to becoming independent young men and women?

Children grow so rapidly. Before you blink, your baby is graduating from high school. How can you store up treasures of their life? Consider keeping a journal filled with stories, sayings, and prayers for your child. Keep a separate one for each child. In the years to come, those precious memories will bring joy to your heart—and theirs.

What memorable event happened in your child's life this past month? Write a short paragraph about that occasion. How did it make you feel? What did that event teach you about your child?

INSPIRATION TO CHANGE: SOUR GRAPES

In the sixth-century B.C., the Babylonians defeated Judah—the southern kingdom of Israel—and carried many Jews, including the prophet Ezekiel, off to Babylon. The Jewish captives were understandably demoralized, and some of them began to quote this proverb, "The fathers eat sour grapes, and the children's teeth are set on edge?" (Ezekiel 18:2 NIV). They considered themselves innocent and accused God of punishing them for the sins of their parents.

Ezekiel 18 records God's reply. In this chapter, God uses three hypothetical generations of one family—a righteous grandfather (verses 5–9), a wicked father (verses 10–13), and a righteous son (verses 14–18)—to emphasize that God holds each individual person responsible for their own sins. While it is true that the sins of parents can result in consequences for future generations, here God affirms that he does not actively "punish" children because of those sins.

Take a moment to think about your childhood. Did you grow up in a Christian home? Were your parents loving and involved? Maybe they were absent or even abusive. Now think about your kids. What is the atmosphere like in which they are growing up?

Let's explore the relationships between the three men God mentions in Ezekiel 18 to see what implications they may have for parents today.

- *No Guarantees*: Even though the grandfather was upright in God's eyes, his son was wicked. Likewise, even if you're right before God and obediently raise your children in a loving home that honors him, that doesn't guarantee your children will follow Christ when they're grown. It certainly improves the probability (2 Timothy 1:5; 3:14–15), but your children are personally accountable to God. Do you have a child who doesn't know God or has strayed? Pray passionately and trust in God. Know that God is actively working to restore that relationship and delights when people return to him (Ezekiel 18:21–23).

- *No Excuses:* Even though the father was evil, his son chose to follow God. Sometimes it's tempting to blame our current situation on our parents. Maybe your father was an alcoholic, or your mother left you when you were young. As hurtful as those events are, God wants you to overcome your past and provide your children with a healthy future. It might seem hard or even impossible, but with God, all things are possible (Mark 10:27). Are you letting the past mistakes of your parents dictate your behavior today? Are you making excuses for your sin?

- *No Life Sentence:* The sins of the father did not dictate the behavior of the son. All parents make mistakes. Some parents are even colossal failures. But in his grace, God does not hold our sins against our children. Maybe you blew it. Be honest, ask God for forgiveness, and ask your child to forgive you as well. Then ask God to help you change. It's not too late to be the father or mother—or grandfather or grandmother—God wants you to be.

DAY 3: PARENTAL "INTERFERENCE"

By today's standards, King David was a super-star. He had a successful career as a warrior and monarch, several best-selling psalms, a hit CD of soothing harp music, and had "man after God's own heart" inscribed on his business cards. Unfortunately, all his endeavors left him with little time to tend to the affairs of his family. In short, King David was a terrible father.

When one of David's sons, Amnon, raped his half-sister, Tamar, David failed to punish him (2 Samuel 13). Tamar's brother, Absalom, didn't think Amnon should get away with it, and had him murdered. Later, Absalom tried to take the throne from David—a move that eventually led to Absalom's death (2 Samuel 18). And another of David's sons, Adonijah, also tried to usurp the throne. One short sentence in Scripture reveals the cause of Adonijah's insurrection and a major flaw in David's parenting technique; "His father had never interfered with him by asking, 'Why do you behave as you do?'" (1 Kings 1:6 NIV).

It is our responsibility, as parents, to discipline our children. We must "interfere" in their lives, and take the time needed to instruct them in the ways of God, to lead them to a greater knowledge of His Word, and to train them to be useful, respectful members of society. When they stray, we should lovingly correct them. If they are defiant, we should punish them. If they show disrespect, we should reprimand them. Failure to take an active part in the training of our children leads to drastic consequences.

Solomon, another of David's sons, wrote, "Discipline your children while there is hope. Otherwise you will ruin their lives" (Proverbs 19:18 NLT). Why be an accomplice to the destruction of our children? Loving discipline helps guide them toward a life of peace that honors God. Like bumpy pavement markers on the highway that caution us when we're drifting into another lane, wise discipline helps keep our children out of harm and headed in the right direction.

Read Hebrews 12:5–11.

In verses 5–6, the author of Hebrews quotes from Proverbs 3:11–12. What are the Lord's discipline and punishment related to? What implication does that have for parents? What does verse 8 say about those who are not disciplined? Why does God discipline us (verse 10)? How should God's example influence the way we discipline our children?

If properly administered, what positive characteristics can discipline produce in our children (verses 9 and 11)? Take some time this week to honestly evaluate your discipline practices. Are you too strict or too lenient? Do your children know why you correct them? Do you primarily view discipline positively, as training, or negatively, as punishment?

> *Kids need to get turned on to new models of self-sacrifice to realize that life is not one big TV show and the plots don't always center on them.*
> —Max Lucado

DAY 4: BLESS YOUR CHILD

During Old Testament times, fathers often prayed a special blessing over their children, particularly before they passed away. These paternal prayers of blessing frequently accompanied the transfer of property and authority and carried profound significance. Isaac's blessing was so valuable, Jacob dressed up in his older brother's clothes and wore goatskin on his hands and neck in order to steal it from Esau (Genesis 27). Later in life, Jacob blessed his twelve sons, a blessing which included the prediction that a royal line would come from Judah (Genesis 49). This prediction was realized in King David and will carry on forever through the Messiah, Jesus Christ.

These prayers of blessing are not a custom that we usually practice today. We might say, "God bless you," when a total stranger sneezes behind us at the bus stop, but how often do we pray God's blessing over our children?

When we bless our children, we are asking for God to give his favor and goodness to them. When we pray God's blessing for our sons and daughters, we entrust them to his divine care, and by doing so, we turn them over to a perfect Father, a trustworthy Parent, and an all-loving God. When we seek God's favor for our children, we ask God to breathe significance into their lives, to make their time on earth productive, and their relationship with Jesus extraordinary.

And as our children listen to our prayers of blessing to God on their behalf, they hear our humble dependence upon him, our genuine concern for their well being, and are reassured of the delight they bring to our lives.

The very existence of your children is evidence of God's blessing in your life (Psalm 127:3–5). Let's ask for God's blessing in theirs.

Read Numbers 6:22–27.

This blessing, often called the Aaronic benediction, is one of the most famous prayers in the Bible, perhaps second only to the Lord's Prayer found in Matthew 6. What do you think it means for the Lord to "make his face shine on you" (for a hint, read Exodus 34:29–35)? How is that different than the Lord "turning his face toward you," which many people have explained as God "smiling" on you?

Who wouldn't want God's blessing, grace, and peace showered upon them? Consider turning verses 24–26 into a blessing that you pray over your children every night. They might think it strange at first, but this tradition will not only keep you focused on what's best for your children, it will also bless them as they listen repeatedly to your heartfelt desire for God's favor in their lives.

In This Together: You Light Up My Life

Someone once said, "What all kids really want is to see their parents light up when they walk in the room." Although it sounds simplistic, it beautifully highlights the truth of unconditional love. Sure, when your daughter is little, it's easy to be enthralled by most everything she does, even when she's naughty. But later, as you watch your teenager struggles with authority, you agonize over the choices she's making. She knows you love her enough to "jump in front of a train" for her, but does she know you're simply glad to see her at the end of the day? In those difficult times, it takes a lot creativity to let a defiant teen know you're still thankful they're part of the family.

Earlier, in the *After The Video* section of this guide, you were asked to spend some time thinking about how parents can show love to their children in the various ways mentioned in 1 Corinthians 13:4–7. You can refer back to your notes on pages 68–70, or jot down your thoughts below.

Love...
is Patient

is Kind

does not Envy

does not Boast

is not Proud

is not Rude

Love...
is not Self-seeking

is not Easily Angered

keeps no Record of Wrongs

does not delight in evil but Rejoices with the Truth

always Protects

always Trusts

always Hopes

always Perseveres

If you are a parent, choose *one* of these love-qualities to put into practice this week. Of course you're always trying to love your kids, but focus especially on this one aspect of love. Try some creative way to show this facet of love.

If your children are already adults, you're not off the hook. You can still show love to them in one of these ways.

If you don't have children, choose someone you know who does have kids and pray for them this week. It might help to choose one of these love-qualities and focus your prayers on that: "Lord, help these parents to have patience in dealing with their kids." (And understand that God sometimes asks us to help answer our own prayers. He might inspire you to offer to babysit, so the parents can have a night off, in case their patience is wearing thin.)

Day 5: An Extravagant Inheritance

The headlines read, "Wealthy Heiress Leaves Pet Dog Millions." Not only did this pampered pooch receive a vast sum of money, she also inherited a jewelry collection fit for the Queen of England and the use of a sprawling mansion, for life. In recent history, stories like this are more frequent than you might expect.

Several words come to mind. Extravagant. Wasteful. Foolish. Half way around the globe, millions of people starve and are without healthy drinking water, while some fluffy canine eats ground filet mignon out of a diamond-encrusted bowl. How quickly we judge the wisdom of leaving a trust fund for a pet.

But how many of us adequately comprehend the extravagance of the inheritance God is preparing for those who believe in his Son? The Apostle John wrote, "How great is the love the Father has lavished on us, that we should be called children of God! And that is what we are!" (1 John 3:1 NIV). Stop. Ponder the significance of that verse. We—mere humans who are created by God in his image but are certainly not gods ourselves—gain eternal life only by God's grace and yet are to be called his children. And as God's children, we will share in the glorious inheritance of heaven (Revelation 21:7). And what an inheritance that will be—streets of pure gold, gates made out of giant pearls, and diamonds and precious stones everywhere (Revelation 21:15–21)! How can this be?

Love. "For God loved the world so much that he gave his one and only Son, so that everyone who believes in him will not perish but have eternal life" (John 3:16 NLT). Our heavenly Father loves us with an unfathomable love—a love so pure and unparalleled that he was willing to sacrifice his Son on the cross so that we might spend eternity with him in a place so spectacular it's beyond our imagination.

Several words come to mind. Extravagant. Grateful. Humbled.

Read Psalm 103:8–14.

In verse 13, God's love for us is compared to a parent's love for a child. Take some time to think about the characteristics of God listed in this passage. He is described as compassionate, gracious, slow to anger, abounding in love, not always accusing, not harboring anger forever, merciful, loving, and forgiving. Which traits best describe you as a parent? Does this list highlight any areas where you can improve?

Part of the reason God shows compassion to us is because he knows how we were made (verse 14). He should, he made us! God has a thorough understanding of the intricacies of our physical, emotional, and spiritual lives. How well do you know your children? This week, spend some focused time getting to know each of your children more deeply.

> *God himself is a father. What parental emotion has he not felt? Are you separated from your child? So was God. Is someone mistreating your child? They mocked and bullied his. Is someone taking advantage of your children? The Son of God was set up by false testimony and betrayed by a greedy follower. Are you forced to watch while your child suffers? God watched his Son on the cross.*
>
> —Max Lucado

WEEK
4

❧ HEREAFTER ❧

Why, you do not even know what will happen tomorrow. What is your life? You are a mist that appears for a little while and then vanishes.

— James 4:14 NIV

❀ INTRODUCTION ❀

Many of us have such busy lives that we don't think much about what's next—until we're forced to. A sudden health scare, an ailing parent, or an untimely death in the neighborhood gets us wondering about the hereafter. Even when we're confident we have a non-stop ticket to heaven, there are still questions about what it's like there, heartaches over those who go before us, and concerns about those we leave behind.

Are you looking forward to heaven with excitement? Some people do, and others feel they should, but many of us are still a bit nervous about the whole heaven thing. It's the Great Unknown. God gives us some glimpses in the Bible, but we're still "seeing through a dark glass." And of course getting there means going through the difficult experience of dying.

So what does the Bible say about life after death? We'll get some answers in this lesson.

❀ ICEBREAKER ❀

What are you looking forward to? Is there some life event you're eagerly anticipating? A vacation, a promotion, getting the kids into school, getting the kids out of school, the start of football season, whatever—what good things are on the horizon for you?

❧ Video Notes ❧

❊ AFTER THE VIDEO ❊

What's your idea of heaven? What do you think it will be like there?

Did Max say anything that surprised you, enlightened you, or disturbed you?

In the first story of this video, we met Smith and Julie, who tragically lost their young son. Smith said, "When you're confronted with someone you love dearly, who an hour prior you were speaking with, and now you're seeing their shell of a body, you begin wrestling with that, and saying, 'Okay, well, where is he? Why would you allow this to happen? Did we do something wrong?' You start down the trail of guilt, shame, and worry." **How would you respond to that? If these grieving parents were friends of yours, what would you tell them?**

Julie talked about opening the Bible and finding pages where her son had scribbled. She said, "I think God used the curiosity inside of me, wanting to know where my son was, to lead me to his loving heart." **What does she mean by that? How does that happen?**

Read Isaiah 57:1–2. **How could this verse help grieving parents?**

In a case like this, the untimely death of someone precious to God, what can we put in each column?

What We Know   What We Don't Know

The second story was told by Gordon, whose neighbor died before he could win him to Christ. He felt terribly guilty about not trying harder. **Has that happened to you? If Gordon was your friend, what would you tell him?**

Once again, we're dealing with some things we know and some things we don't know. **In a case like this, when a neighbor died before they could lead him to Christ, what do we know and what don't we know?**

<u>What We Know</u>   <u>What We Don't Know</u>

How does someone get to heaven? Do we know this?

But what *don't* we know in this situation?

Does it mean we don't have to tell our neighbors about Jesus?

Read 1 Peter 1:3-6. There are many Bible passages that talk about heaven. But we're going to take a quick look at a few passages that tell us how to live in the expectation of heaven. Verse 3 says we've been born into a "living hope." **What does that mean? What is a "living hope"?**

How does the hope of heaven affect the way you live? As you go through life *this week*, what difference will it make?

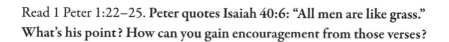

Read 1 Peter 1:22–25. Peter quotes Isaiah 40:6: "All men are like grass." What's his point? How can you gain encouragement from those verses?

Verse 22 exhorts us to "love one another deeply, from the heart." What does that have to do with eternal existence? It's a lovely exhortation; how does it fit here?

Read 2 Peter 3:3–4. What are the "scoffers" saying? Do you find that same sort of attitude these days? How does that affect your "living hope" of heaven?

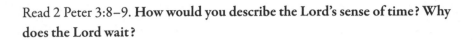

Read 2 Peter 3:8–9. **How would you describe the Lord's sense of time? Why does the Lord wait?**

Read John 14:1–6. **How do you feel when you hear these verses?**

How have you been affected by this four-week *Max on Life* study? Share one thing this study has caused you to think about more deeply and one thing you are going to do differently from now on.

> "... who by the power that enables him to bring everything under his control, will transform our lowly bodies so that they will be like his glorious body."
> (Philippians 3:21 NIV)

❀ REFLECTIVE READING ❀

DAY 1: THE PRODUCTION DESIGNER

Millions of moviegoers sat spellbound as tall blue creatures rode atop flying Banshees through the floating mountains of Pandora. *Avatar's* success was due, in part, to the dazzling world created by James Cameron and his team of Production Designers and Art Directors. Their fanciful planet exploded with bioluminescent plants and animals—floating wood sprites, lizards that unfurled like fans and spiraled away to safety, and large-leafed plants that coiled up in response to touch. Critics marveled at their creativity.

But as inventive as they were, do you think their imagination rivals that of the Infinite Creator? Genesis 1 affirms that God created the whole universe simply by speaking it into existence. No team of digital effects artists. No multi-million dollar computer render farm. God didn't place virtual lights in a virtual set; God hung the stars in the sky and carefully positioned the sun an ideal distance from planet earth. The snow-capped Alps, the dense rainforests of Brazil, the clean-swept beaches of Fiji—they were all his idea. And as awe-inspiring as this world is, God isn't finished—there's more.

The Bible tells us that God is preparing a new heaven and a new earth—a place he and his followers will inhabit forever (John 14:3; Revelation 21:1; 22:5). It will be a place of unfathomable beauty—where what is currently extraordinary becomes ordinary (Revelation 21:15–21). Gold is as common as asphalt and diamonds as prevalent as concrete. If we, God's creation, can dream up places like Pandora, the forest moon of Endor, and Middle-earth's Rivendell, imagine what God has in store?

The Divine Production Designer is at work on a sequel—and it's one you won't want to miss.

Read Revelation 21:1–22:6.

John records a description of a city, the New Jerusalem, in verses 10 to 27. As you read this section, there are several characteristics of the city listed—it is secure, safe and accessible, extravagant, super-abounding in blessings, and unparalleled in prestige. Compared to the world today, what do these characteristics tell you about heaven?

In Revelation 22:2, John notes the presence of the tree of life. Think back to Genesis 3. What tree found in the Garden of Eden is missing in heaven? Why do you think that's significant?

Carefully re-read Revelation 21:3–7. What do these verses tell you about God? How is that different from our current situation? What things are absent in heaven?

> *God dangles a Yosemite waterfall or Caribbean coast in our direction and says, "This is just a sample of what awaits you. The best of this world is a postcard of the next." The earth is God's hors d'oeuvre tray.*
> —Max Lucado

DAY 2: JESUS WINS

Ask most Christians which individual books of the Bible they've read the least, and the Book of Revelation will probably be near the top of the list—right by Obadiah and Leviticus. Part of the reluctance to read Revelation comes from its difficult symbolism. Scholars have disagreed for centuries over the meaning of the book, and it seems like every few years someone announces they've "cracked the code." A book gets published explaining the precise time of Christ's return, the identity of the Antichrist, and why locusts represent helicopters. We wonder, "If Revelation has the 'professionals' stumped, how are the rest of us supposed to figure it out?" But to view Revelation as a cryptogram to be deciphered is to entirely miss the main point.

Near the end of the first-century A.D., the Roman Emperor Domitian demanded that people worship him as a god. This decree clearly violated God's command to worship him alone, so many Christians refused. As a result, the early Christian church experienced significant persecution. The Romans exiled the Apostle John to the island of Patmos, from which he wrote the Book of Revelation (Revelation 1:9). John wrote to seven churches located in modern-day Turkey—churches that were suffering for their belief in Jesus Christ (Revelation 1:9–11).

In infinite wisdom and grace, God delivers to John a vision of his ultimate plan for humanity. God skips to the last chapter of time and reveals its stunning conclusion. This Jesus, for whom people are suffering, will return to earth. He will come back, not as the suffering servant, but as a triumphant King. He will conquer evil and establish his Kingdom, and those who have placed their faith in him will reign with him forever (Revelation 22:5). Imagine the hope this message gave those early Christians who were suffering for Christ.

Simply put, the main message of Revelation is that Jesus wins. And if you believe in him, so do you.

Read Revelation 1:3.

While all Scripture is profitable (2 Timothy 3:16), Revelation is the only book that includes a specific blessing to those who read, hear, and obey its words. Why do you think God decided to include this blessing in Revelation? What does that tell you about the importance of reading this final book of the Bible? Make it a goal to read a chapter a day for the next 22 days.

Read Revelation 2:8–11.

This is one of the letters to the seven churches. What truth about Jesus does John include in verse 8? God tells the church in Smyrna that he knows about their suffering. How does God encourage them to respond, and what promise does he make (verse 10)? How can these verses encourage you in your present situation?

INSPIRATION TO CHANGE: LOVE IS ETERNAL

First Corinthians 13 includes some of the most famous words ever written about love. In this chapter, the Apostle Paul tells us that nothing we do matters without love (verses 1–3). After defining love (verses 4–7) and establishing its permanence (verses 8–12), Paul concludes, "And now these three remain: faith, hope and love. But the greatest of these is love" (1 Corinthians 13:13 NIV).

Have you ever wondered why love is greater than faith and hope? Scripture defines faith as "being sure of what we hope for and certain of what we do not see" (Hebrews 11:1 NIV). We know that "without faith it is impossible to please God" (Hebrews 11:6 NIV). And without faith in Jesus Christ, no one enters heaven (Ephesians 2:8–9). Faith is monumentally important.

And what about hope? Hope is confident expectation about what is to come (Romans 8:24–25). Before Christ saved us we had no hope (Ephesians 2:12), but now we can boldly place our hope in "the glorious appearing of our great God and Savior, Jesus Christ" (Titus 2:13 NIV). This life would be unbearable without hope.

So why does love trump faith and hope? Because love lasts forever. Imagine that day when you stand before Jesus Christ in heaven. You are finally able to see your Savior with your own eyes—your faith has become sight. And as you experience your new disease-free body and throw your arms around your baby girl who died before her third birthday, you realize that your hope has now been realized. But love remains.

Are you pursuing a life defined by love? How are you at loving your spouse? Your kids? God? Do you love others enough to share the good news of eternal salvation found only in Jesus Christ? Everything you do in love lasts *forever*.

Day 3: Reward Cards

It seems like almost every business in existence these days offers rewards. You get rewarded for buying gas, groceries, and pet food. You're asked to swipe your reward card at the electronics store and pharmacy. They even make mini cards you attach to your keychain—so you'll never miss what's coming to you. And on top of that, a leading video game manufacturer rewards you for all your "time and dedication" spent playing hours of their games. But is being compensated for buying Cheerios or for racking up the highest score on Madden NFL really the kinds of rewards we should pursue?

Jesus said, "For the Son of Man is going to come in his Father's glory with his angels, and then he will reward each person according to what he has done" (Matthew 16:27 NIV). Scripture affirms that Christ will reward us all according to our deeds (Revelation 22:12; 2 Corinthians 5:10). Our deeds do not get us into heaven, because salvation is a free gift granted by God's grace to those who have faith in Jesus Christ (Ephesians 2:8–9). But what we do during our time on earth does matter to God. The Apostle Paul wrote, "For we are God's workmanship, created in Christ Jesus *to do good works,* which God prepared in advance for us to do" (Ephesians 2:10 NIV, emphasis added).

What good works does God have in mind? The Bible mentions that there will be rewards for enduring suffering and persecution for Jesus' sake (Matthew 5:12), for giving and praying in secret (Matthew 6:4, 6), for offering someone a cup of water (Mark 9:41), for loving our enemies (Luke 6:35), and for doing good (Ephesians 6:8). God rewards acts of humble love and service to others (Matthew 25:31–46).

The next time you jingle your keys, consider how many points you've stored up on your heavenly reward card.

Read 1 Corinthians 3:10–15.

What is the "foundation" that all our good deeds must be built upon (verse 11)? Look at the list of "building materials" in verse 12. Do you think they represent the quality of work done or the motive behind the work, or both? What is "the Day" in verse 13 (see 2 Corinthians 5:10)? How do we know that Paul is talking about eternal rewards and not eternal salvation (verses 14–15)?

Take some time to consider what foundation you are building on. How much of your time is spent trying to gain earthly rewards? How intentional are you about focusing on doing good works that lead to heavenly rewards? Do you think it's wrong to serve someone with the motive of gaining an eternal reward? Why or why not?

> *For all we don't know about the next life, this much is certain. The day Christ comes will be a day of reward. Those who went unknown on earth will be known in heaven. Those who never heard the cheers of people will hear the cheers of angels. Those who missed the blessing of a father will hear the blessing of their heavenly Father.*
>
> —Max Lucado

Day 4: This Same Jesus

And just like that, he was gone. The small band of disciples huddled together, eyes straining, heads raised toward heaven. Their leader—the man they watched die a painful death only to be resurrected three days later, the man they spent the last forty days with in stunned amazement—had just vanished through the clouds. Suddenly two men glowing white appeared next to them and said, "Why do you stand here looking into the sky? This *same Jesus*, who has been taken from you into heaven, will come back in the same way you have seen him go into heaven" (Acts 1:11 NIV, emphasis added).

Jesus will return. The very same God-man who walked the face of this earth two thousand years ago, who raised a widow's only son up from the dead—not because anyone asked him to but out of his great compassion, who gave sight to the blind and hearing to the deaf, who calmed the storms and healed the lepers, who cast out demons and walked on water, *this same Jesus* is coming back.

But much will also be different. When the Son of God arrived the first time, he came as a baby in a manger. When he returns, he comes as the King on a white stallion. A great company of angels heralded his birth; at his second coming, he's bringing *all* the angels. His initial visit largely went unnoticed; no one will miss his return. Although blameless, he was judged and found guilty; in perfection, he will judge all and pronounce guilt. He quietly endured crucifixion by those who sought to destroy him; he will war against his enemies and vanquish them. He came to serve, he returns to reign. He came to die, he returns to destroy death. He came to bear our sins, he returns to bring salvation.

Yes, this same Jesus will return, but nothing else will ever be the same.

Read Daniel 7:13–14.

Who is the "Ancient of Days"? Who is the "one like a son of man" (verse 13)? What is the significance of him "coming with the clouds" (see Revelation 1:7)? What was he given (verse 14)? Who worshiped him? What are the characteristics of his kingdom? How do these verses compare to Ephesians 1:20–23?

The Book of Daniel was written over 2,500 years ago. What does the prophecy in these verses tell you about God and his plan? What difference does that make in your life? Spend some time this week thinking about what it will be like to live forever under King Jesus. How does what you know about Jesus' life on earth 2,000 years ago impact your understanding of what heaven will be like?

In This Together: Your Tour of Duty

Whether we like it or not, we are all part of a cosmic crusade between good and evil. Fortunately, we know which side wins. Jesus and his armies will defeat Satan and his followers and banish them forever (Revelation 20:7–15). But while we eagerly wait for Christ's ultimate victory, the war on earth wages on. Right now, Satan and his band of fallen angels scour the earth hunting for souls to devour (1 Peter 5:8). But they do not advance unopposed. God has commissioned angels to resist the devil's troops (Daniel 10:13), and as followers of Jesus Christ, we too have been enlisted in the fight.

That's why the Apostle Paul instructs us to put on the full armor of God (Ephesians 6:10–20). In his grace, God doesn't leave us to fight evil on our own. He provides us with truth, righteousness, peace, faith, salvation, His Word, and even Himself—the Holy Spirit alive in each believer. And while these weapons help us defend ourselves, they are also meant to assist us as we launch an offensive.

But what are we to invade? Before Jesus left this earth, he gave specific instructions. "Go and make disciples of all the nations, baptizing them in the name of the Father and the Son and the Holy Spirit. Teach these new disciples to obey all the commands I have given you. And be sure of this: I am with you always, even to the end of the age" (Matthew 28:19–20 NLT). These are our combat orders.

Our directive is clear—invade the enemy territory with the good news of Jesus Christ. Our ally is divine— we bring the message, but the Holy Spirit alone draws people to God. And the consequences are eternal—for when our Commanding Officer returns, the battle is over.

Your Mission This Week: Talk about heaven with someone. It could be a family discussion at the dinner table. You could study some of the Bible verses mentioned in this guide with a friend. Chat with another Christian about what you're most looking forward to in heaven. Or raise the subject with an unbelieving friend and listen to what they think about life after death.

> *I have found that people who say they want nothing to do with Christ sometimes do. Their outward defenses say no, but their inner heart says yes.*
> —Max Lucado

DAY 5: PERFECTION

Do you remember the Milton Bradley game *Perfection*? It's been making kids of all ages jump out of their skin for over thirty-five years. You'd flip a switch and then race like mad to fit all the twenty-five different geometric shapes into the right holes before the timer went off. If you didn't make it, the tray would violently pop up and fling little plastic pieces around the room and your heart into your throat. Part of the rush was the sense of urgency you felt as you tried to beat the clock. You really had to get busy, because you knew it would all be over in sixty seconds.

Life's kind of like *Perfection*—we too need to get busy since time is running out. One day, life as we know it will end. Jesus will return to earth and establish his kingdom forever. *But when?* The disciples asked Jesus that exact question and he told them, "No one knows about that day or hour, not even the angels in heaven, nor the Son, but only the Father" (Matthew 24:36 NIV). And while Father God alone knows the moment of Jesus' return, the Bible affirms that it could happen at any time (1 Thessalonians 5:2).

How should knowing that Christ could return at any moment affect the way we live? One group of Christians decided to quit their jobs, hang out at home, and stare into the sky. The Apostle Paul had strong words for them. He told them to get busy, to pull their own weight! Christ's return isn't an excuse to be idle; it should motivate us to encourage one another, to work hard at our careers, to share the good news of salvation in Jesus, and to never get tired of doing what is right (1 Thess 5:1–11; 2 Thess 3:6–15). All of human history marches toward that moment when Jesus Christ will return. But until he does, we must faithfully and diligently perform the tasks he has for us to do.

Some day the tray will pop up. And then, everyone who believes in Jesus will be made perfect.

Read Matthew 25:14–30.

In Matthew 24–25, Jesus talks about the end of the age and his coming Kingdom. This parable of the talents gives us information about how we are to live before Christ's return, and the impact our earthy lives will have on eternity. What does verse 15 tell us about what God gives us and what he expects? Will we be held accountable for what God entrusts to us (verse 19)? How will what we do on earth affect our lives in heaven (verses 21, 23)?

The Master will return. What are you doing with what God has entrusted to you?

> *Jesus' imminent return does not give us permission to give up but is an invitation to get busy. There's work to be done, because when Jesus returns, that's it. The final finale. The tolling of the bell.*
> —Max Lucado

❧ SPECIAL THANKS ❧
TO OUR HOST BRIAN MOSLEY

I am the President of RightNow and Bluefish TV. Our team loves serving the church with Bible Study video curriculum. You can also check out our RightNow Conference for church leaders and RightNow Training for on demand, online small group training.

I married my high school sweetheart, Julie. We have three kids, Abby, Grant and Ashley. As licensed foster parents, our home is sometimes a little fuller. We worship and serve at Allen Bible Church where I am also an elder.

Brian Mosley